A GUIDE TO
COMMERCIAL PROPERTY CONVERSION

Special 3rd Edition

MAKE BIG MONEY BY TURNING LESS VALUABLE COMMERCIAL PROPERTY INTO MORE VALUABLE RESIDENTIAL PROPERTIES

Powerful Techniques anyone can use to replace their salary and escape the rat race quickly.

This book shows you how to invest even if you have none of your own money to invest.

Sumit Gupta

AssocRICS B.Com (Hons) PGDBA (FINANCE) MBA (INTERNATIONAL BUSINESS)

An entrepreneur, Author, Property Investor, Mentor & International Speaker

Presented by:

Global Property Consulting

GUIDE TO COMMERCIAL PROPERTY CONVERSIONS
SPECIAL 3RD EDITION

Disclaimer

The information in this book is for education purpose only. The contents do not constitute financial and legal advice in any way. You should seek independent professional advice before making any investment.

This book is available online, kindle, our centres and in Book stores.

GUIDE TO COMMERCIAL PROPERTY CONVERSIONS
SPECIAL 3RD EDITION

Table of Contents

Acknowledgements 4

Prologue 8

Chapter 1: Introduction 15

Chapter 2: Why to invest in property 32

Chapter 3: What is Commercial Property 44

Chapter 4: Why do Commercial Conversion 47

Chapter 5: Prior Approval Vs. Full Planning 52

Chapter 6: New Permitted Development Law 2020 65

Chapter 7: Commercial Property Conversion Model 78

Chapter 8: Construciton Project Management Essentials 87

Chapter 9: Title Splitting and Maximusing Profit 95

Chapter 10: The best investment 99

About Sumit Gupta 112

GUIDE TO COMMERCIAL PROPERTY CONVERSIONS
SPECIAL 3RD EDITION

ACKNOWLEDGEMENTS

I would not be the person I am today without the love, support and influence of many people.

To my beautiful wife Poonam, you are my soul mate and support. I am so grateful for the tireless work and great caring you give to me and our kids.

To my children Yash and Arnav, you're all unique and amazingly great. I am proud to be your Dad. You bring joy and purpose to my life. Thank you for being my reason to strive and be alive.

I acknowledge the souls that are no longer here such as Mahatma Gandhi, Nelson Mandela, Steve Jobs for having such a positive impact on me and the humanity.

I am grateful for the leadership of her Majesty The Queen, Donald Trump, Narendra Modi, and many others whom I have not named but who continue to tirelessly help make the world a better place for me and many others around the world.

I acknowledge some of the great business minds that I have had pleasure of learning from and being associated with such some of them like warren buffet, Sir Richard Branson, Laud sugar, Robert

GUIDE TO COMMERCIAL PROPERTY CONVERSIONS
SPECIAL 3RD EDITION

Kiyosaki, Tony Robins, T Harv Eker, Les Brown and Dr John Demartini.

To my Spiritual Guru, SRI SRI Ravi Shankar who has helped me throughout my life to be a better human being. Your taught meditation techniques made me a better person, helped me to maintain the centeredness in any difficult situation and keeping calm mind. These techniques really help me in anything I do in my life and help me to have better productivity, sharpness and creativity.

I acknowledge the Art of Living Foundation for the spiritual and amazing work they are doing in uplifting humanity.

Finally, I acknowledge you for receiving this book and using it in the most positive way that you know.

GUIDE TO COMMERCIAL PROPERTY CONVERSIONS
SPECIAL 3RD EDITION

SEVEN UNIVERSAL TRUTHS

Truth No. 1

Everything and I mean everything you want to achieve begins with a thought. So allow yourself the time and space to daydream, visualize, and use your imagination to craft the most amazing scenarios of what you want your life to be.

Truth No. 2

No matter where you are in your life, you will always be able to come up with an excuse to wait.

Truth No. 3

Everything that has happened in your life, whether good or bad, has happened for a reason. Your experience have gifted you a unique empathy with people who face what you faced.

Truth No. 4

The knowledge, know-how and experience you have acquired to date are valuable asset. The most important investment you can make is in yourself.

GUIDE TO COMMERCIAL PROPERTY CONVERSIONS
SPECIAL 3RD EDITION

Truth No. 5

The world has changed. You no longer need to be skilled & experienced and allowing an employer to capitalise on that knowledge and wisdom you get paid fraction of what they are making out of you.

Truth No. 6

You can reach thousands if not millions of people using social media and internet outreach.

Truth No. 7

If you want different results, you have to do things differently.

If any of these truths have resonated with you and if you have not done so already, please invest in this book and I will reveal to you the strategies for property investment step by steps.

SUMIT

Sumit Gupta

But before we begin our journey together, there is something I think you ought to know.....

PROLOGUE

Have you ever had dreamt to achieve something really BIG in your life? Yes, even I did?

If you were with me around November 2004 in India city called Mumbai, you would have found me very slowly entering through a door. I am seeing him sitting on a sofa watching TV, a dark place and light flickering. He is around 5.10 feet tall with white hair. His piercing eyes are looking like typical father. He asked me where were you until this late night.

I was like what do I say, how will he react. He says "Is this a time to come home, its 11pm" I said "Dad, I attended a seminar where I met a guy who was teaching dream big, become rich, learn and earn in UK"

Dad "that is not for you son. They all are crook".

I "No, this sounds so appealing; I do not want to do a job like this for rest of my life".

GUIDE TO COMMERCIAL PROPERTY CONVERSIONS
SPECIAL 3RD EDITION

Dad "what's wrong with you, you have a secure job working for Standard chartered bank"

I "Dad, secure job? Job is not my future. I want to do something bigger and better in my life. See I read this book *Rich Dad Poor Dad*, Robert teaches about investment. My salary is not enough to save enough, how do I invest?" "Dad I've decided to go to UK to do further study and work, I will earn lots of money and do something better with my life"

Dad "Son, do not mess up with your secure job & future and anyways I do not have money to give you. These people show big dream to sell their products". I said "NN...No dad.....He said "just shut up... end of discussion".

I am like, I have decided so I will have to do it somehow. Just to cut my story short, after few months of great struggle & lots of efforts, lots of argument with family, I managed to turn this impossible looking task possible. I took out all my savings from the bank, encashed my PF funds, sold whatever I could and still could get only 20% of my UK study fee. To overcome this hurdle I then borrowed the rest from the bank, resigned my bank job and came to UK; effectively with lots of debts and enchased

GUIDE TO COMMERCIAL PROPERTY CONVERSIONS
SPECIAL 3RD EDITION

almost everything I had in India and left my so-called secured job.

After paying all my course fee and flight tickets etc., I was left with some little change when I arrived in London. While I was in flight on my way to London, I was thinking in my head what if I do not get a job immediately after landing to London how do I survive? Initially when I came to London for first few months, I was only eating one time in a day, could not sleep well, not just because of hunger but also hunger to achieve something big. I was doing some odd part time jobs.

Then finally, I got a proper office job in an Estate Agency. I started to gain further qualifications in real estate and got 5 certified qualifications one after other. Then this day comes around mid-2008 after the crash when employers were sacking or reducing their staffs. I faced similar threat and I was bit worried and thinking what shall I do now, stay here in London or go back home. All sorts of thoughts were going in my mind. Was my father correct? By Saying we are lower middle class people we cannot dream to become rich. The following morning I woke up with heavy heart and sat for meditation that

GUIDE TO COMMERCIAL PROPERTY CONVERSIONS
SPECIAL 3RD EDITION

I only used to do when I used to get upset not like regularly as I do now a days. While meditating, I am questing in my mind why did I come to UK? Shall I go back or stay here? My guru Sri Sri appears in my mind ... he said "Sumit it's not about the country. It's about you. You got to do things differently if you want different result." I decided in that moment I will do things differently now. I sat down and thought what skills do I have, Post-graduation degree in finance, Qualified Surveyor and legally sound personality who fought over 100s of cases in court, tribunal, high court etc. I decided to set up a consultancy business. With my multi-skill of finance, legal and property skills I was helping my investors clients to buy properties arranging funding for them. Slowly things started to change one by one, and I was getting good at what I was doing day by day. I was helping my investor clients to build millions of pound worth portfolio. I was nominated for best negotiator award. I was one of the surveyors who challenged and took deviation against some precedent cases like sportily V Cadagon and won. I defeated Canterbury council on a prohibition order made for 10 sq. meter studio flat which is probably the smallest self-

GUIDE TO COMMERCIAL PROPERTY CONVERSIONS
SPECIAL 3RD EDITION

containted unit you could have ever seen in UK, and many more record-breaking cases. One day I attended a property seminar watching the presenter explaining about few investment strategies. And while listening them, I was like oh yes on my Croydon deal I used this strategy and on that Brixton deal I used this strategy. I found that these property trainer are making lots of money teaching about property investment strategies and they do not know various strategies that I know like adding value to property without even physically touching the property, creatively buying from auctions etc. Because I can do finance and tax planning and I am legally sound, I can go extra mile comparatively. Then I become more creative, I decided not to ask some of my clients for fee whom I was getting great BMV and development potential deals but I started to ask them share in profit or equity in property. By doing so soon in less than 15 months, I found myself financial free, having a multi-million pound worth property portfolio without using any of my own money. In additional to that I helped many of my investor partners to build their multi-million pound property portfolio. I phoned my dad and said "Dad, we do not need money to fulfil

GUIDE TO COMMERCIAL PROPERTY CONVERSIONS
SPECIAL 3RD EDITION

our dreams, we need to be resourceful, determined and laser focused."

I started to share with my friends and clients some of my work experience and successful deals that I did. And I found they were getting impressed with performance and they asked me "can you teach us these investment strategies". I said yes sure and then I decided to educate others to do the same what I have done. With over 17 years of experience and multi-skilled I designed various training programs, books and courses to help people to achieve financial freedom and be successful. My training programs not only help my students / mentee to build their property portfolio but also teach them soft skills to empower their life. I designed some very easy steps SYSTEM, it's as easy as I make the cake in front of you and you can see me doing and then you just follow my recipe to get the same result. "SUCCESS LEAVES CLUES"

"WHY FIT IN, WHEN YOU WERE BORN TO STAND OUT"

GUIDE TO COMMERCIAL PROPERTY CONVERSIONS
SPECIAL 3RD EDITION

CHAPTER 1: INTRODUCTION

"People with goals succeed because they know where they're going." — Earl Nightingale

If you are reading this book, chances are you have already started your own business or investment, or perhaps you are still gathering information in order to take that first step. But let me ask you a few questions: What do you want to get by investing into property? Do you want financial freedom? The ability to spend your time and money in the way you want rather than being tied to your regular 9 to 5 (but you always end up staying until 8) job?

Do you want to be the millionaire? I assume your answer must be yes. Why not, everyone likes to become millionaire but who actually accomplish those desires.

Why is that? The answer is simple: Most people do not apply six very common principles to their efforts when buying and selling property:

1. If you expect to have someone else do all of the work for you, do not expect that you will receive all of the rewards—**learn what to do and then get it done!**

GUIDE TO COMMERCIAL PROPERTY CONVERSIONS
SPECIAL 3RD EDITION

2. Don't believe everything that you read or that you are told, unless you check it out for yourself—**you must be self-sufficient!**
3. If you don't have a map to get you where you want to go, you probably won't ever get there—**you must have a plan!**
4. If you do not ask for a better deal, you probably won't get it—**so always ask**
5. Those that snooze will lose and you cannot wait. Once you know what to do—**you must go out and make it happen!**
6. And most important—never forget! It does not take money to make money, it takes a deal to make money.

I assume you would agree with me that investment is very important to be successful, then why do people refuse to invest? Perhaps they do not have enough time, knowledge or they have fear to invest.

Probably fear is only until when you have not learned how to invest in property. Once you learn the skills, you will feel more confidents to invest in property.

GUIDE TO COMMERCIAL PROPERTY CONVERSIONS
SPECIAL 3RD EDITION

Here are few Property Investment Top Tips, we will learn more about them in this book

1. Always Buy from motivated sellers at BMV (below market Value)
2. Always Buy in an area that have strong demand
3. Always Buy for good cash flow
4. Always Invest for long term
5. Always maintain enough working capital
6. Always do proper due diligence
7. Always Think creatively and Add Value
8. Always Leverage with other's money, time and experience
9. Always Make a team of professional people
10. Always keep up to date with latest legislation

Before we go further, I want you to understand few basics first. It is good to get the foundation level develop first before we look to develop anything.

✓ Clearly Identify Exactly What You Want to Achieve

Everyone has dreams. Unfortunately, most people never achieve much, if any, of what they dream. Why do you suppose that is?

GUIDE TO COMMERCIAL PROPERTY CONVERSIONS
SPECIAL 3RD EDITION

As a seminar instructor, for many years I have travelled many countries around the world and had the opportunity to spend time helping many people build fortunes in real estate. In most respects, these people are just like many of you reading this book. In their lives, they had done many of the things that you do every day. They went to work, they cooked, they went to sports, they took the kids to school, they went to the health club, and they shopped for groceries.... Sound familiar, right?

However, ultimately, there is a difference between the people who become very successful and the rest of the world. Successful people are successful because they do the things they like the most. The most! Let me explain. People go to work day after day and many of them don't really care for their jobs. The job is not what they most like to do. Frankly, almost all of them would rather be doing something different, be paid more, have more time off, have better benefits, have more freedom—and the list goes on and on. So why do they stay where they are? The answer can be explained in three words: security, procrastination, and fear!

GUIDE TO COMMERCIAL PROPERTY CONVERSIONS
SPECIAL 3RD EDITION

- ✓ Security because they at least have a job and don't really have to make a change.
- ✓ Procrastination because they want to change, but never quite gets around to it.
- ✓ Fear because they might be worse off if they do make a change.

Let me ask you few questions?

Are they really secure? What's the security in job? How many companies have closed their doors? How many thousands of people have lost their jobs?

Remember this: Your own personal security can only exist when you can independently generate whatever income you desire and your future is totally in your control. And what could be the biggest fear in life beyond death. We all came empty handed and we all will die without taking anything with us. Why not live the life fully, use all the resources and perform the way the world will remember us.

"Living life fully is like a roller coaster ride. There is a whirling, spinning, fast-paced perceptions, and adventure! If you are tense and holding on tight, resisting each turn, you will

feel exhausted and sick at the end. But if you can relax and have faith that the builder of the ride made it for your fun and safety, then you feel thrilled, energized, and joyful!"

GOALS — The Most Valuable Building Blocks

"Goal setting," you groan, "not that again. Every time I read a book or watch a video or go to a seminar, they talk about how important it is to set goals."

Yes, and once again, I will tell you what you have already heard 10 or 100 or 1000 times: Setting concise but flexible goals, writing them down, continually reviewing those goals, and measuring your accomplishments is critical to your own success!

- ✓ Like it or not, it is an absolute necessity. Right now is a good time to begin asking yourself: What exactly do I want to achieve out of this new real estate investment book?
- ✓ Do you want to build an on-going, income-generating business at which you can work full time?
- ✓ Do you want to keep your current job and begin buying and selling periodically for either additional income or a more fruitful retirement?

GUIDE TO COMMERCIAL PROPERTY CONVERSIONS
SPECIAL 3RD EDITION

- ✓ Do you simply want to become a real estate mogul and buy and hold as many properties as possible to secure your future?
- ✓ Do you just want to buy your first house?

Identifying your goals is very important for many reasons. Most importantly, because you will learn many, many techniques from this book, it is important that you utilize the information that will best suit your needs and desires. It may take you years to utilize every method that will be shown to you. Concentrating on a specific plan and specific methods will provide the best results. As you become more and more knowledgeable and proficient with the techniques, the entire process will become less cumbersome and you will be able to branch out and use other methods.

However, remember that your goals also need to be reasonable and flexible. Reasonable, in that you must honestly evaluate the time and resources that you have to put into your own property investing venture. Flexible, because you may start out with a goal to only buy your first house and find that the process was so easy that you want to buy several more. Setting the goals,

GUIDE TO COMMERCIAL PROPERTY CONVERSIONS
SPECIAL 3RD EDITION

measuring your achievements, and moving the bar up to the next level is the progression of success in nearly every venture in life. The investment goal chart will help you break down each of the actions that you will need to take to accomplish your aspirations. Note that the chart requires you to state a goal, show the action that will be required, and then break down the specific actions that will be necessary.

One example might be:

Investment Goal: To purchase two properties within 90 days
Actions:

- ✓ Search the ads for properties online and offline
- ✓ Contact a Estate Agent and have her or him searched
- ✓ Search repossessed and run down properties including properties going in auction room
- ✓ Drive around the area and look for "For Sale by Owner" signs
- ✓ Specific Actions: Contact a minimum of 20 sellers, do follow-up letters to sellers, and view at least six properties within a set time say within a week.

Broker contact: identify 20 potential properties and view a minimum of six properties a week or more.

GUIDE TO COMMERCIAL PROPERTY CONVERSIONS
SPECIAL 3RD EDITION

Driving around and

- ✓ Identify a minimum of four sellers, view a minimum of two properties,
- ✓ offers on two properties and negotiate

By breaking down your goals in this manner, you will know the exact actions that you need to take every day to accomplish your goals.

It also is very important to segregate your goals into four categories:

1. Daily action goals
2. Short-term achievement goals
3. Mid-term achievement goals
4. Long-term success goals

GUIDE TO COMMERCIAL PROPERTY CONVERSIONS
SPECIAL 3RD EDITION

Daily Action Goals

These goals can best be defined as daily, weekly, and monthly activities such as personal contacts with potential sellers, viewing properties, creating and distributing flyers, and follow-ups on potential deals— everyday activities that will be necessary for you to find and close the transactions that will allow you to achieve your short-term achievement goals. Daily action goals will become almost second nature, but you must continue to track your results or you may become scattered and disorganized. Time is your most important asset and setting and prioritizing specific daily action goals will help you to utilize your time most efficiently.

Short-Term Achievement Goals

These are those goals that you want to achieve in one year or less. These include making a monthly or annual income, paying off bills, buying one or two or three properties, taking a certain vacation, buying a new car, creating more time to spend with your family, quitting your job and working full time in real estate, etc. Short-term achievement goals are the stepping stones that move you sequentially closer to achieving your long-term success goals.

Mid-Term Achievement Goals

These are those goals that you want to achieve in two years to 5 years. Some examples of five-year mid-term success goals might be net worth of £1 million, ownership of 20 properties producing a net income of £100,000 a year etc.

Long-Term Success Goals

These are those goals that you want to achieve in 5 to 10 years. Ten-year goals can be moved up substantially, but keep in mind, things change. Your 5 to and 10 year long-term success goals need to be the most flexible.

As you gain more knowledge, experience, and confidence, you also will become smarter at setting goals and you'll find that you have a tendency to push yourself a little more than you did when you were first beginning your new venture. As I said before, as you work with the process, the easier it will become and the less complicated it will seem to you. It will be the same with your goal setting. It will become habitual and second nature. Our minds need to have clear WHY to function and achieve the goal.

GUIDE TO COMMERCIAL PROPERTY CONVERSIONS
SPECIAL 3RD EDITION

We should have our clear written down goals, that you read every day before you start your day and plan what action will you take today to achieve that goal.

Once Harvard's graduate students were asked if they had set themselves any goals and if so, if they had made any plans to accomplish them

Group A: 3% had written down goals with plans to accomplish them

Group B: 13% had goals and plans in mind but with nothing written down

Group C: 84% had no goals at all

After 10 years they revisited the same group of students and the results were very clear...

Group B: Earned on average twice as much as Group C

Group A: Earned on average 10 times as much as all of Group B and Group C combined!

See the power of having a written goal.

Time—Your Most Valuable Asset

How many times have you heard someone say, "I would love to be able to have the time to do this or that or be able to go here

GUIDE TO COMMERCIAL PROPERTY CONVERSIONS
SPECIAL 3RD EDITION

or there, but I am so busy and have so little time that I just can't do it." Many of you have probably said or thought those same things at one time or another. But, the real truth is that there are only 24 hours in a day and we all make the time that we need or want to for the things that are the real priorities in our lives. If you want something different than what you have, you must first, and honestly, change your priorities. We all have the same amount of time each and every single day. We spend the time, we waste the time or invest the time creatively. What we do with our time is entirely up to us.

Many people enjoy looking and acting and being busy. The problem is that most people are highly unproductive, whether they are busy or not. Like any other venture, if you are to be successful in the property investment business, you must prioritize and manage your time to allow you to complete the actions that will be necessary for you to achieve your goals. Remember, a commitment of four or five hours a week might be all that is necessary for you to become a successful property investor.

GUIDE TO COMMERCIAL PROPERTY CONVERSIONS
SPECIAL 3RD EDITION

Work smartly and see how you spend your time every day, record in a diary and see what are the task you can outsource to others at a cheaper rate than what you are worth. These days you can get almost anything done through others using fiverr, upwork, peopleperhour type platform. You spend your time in what is really necessary and invest your time in your personal development as much as possible.

Managing Your Time

There have been many books written on time management. Here is my simple, two-part formula for successful time management, broken into preparation and actions.

Preparation

Simplify your life. Stop doing the things that are not essential or that you really don't want or have to do the things that are getting in the way of the success that you want to achieve.

Control what people and actions get your time. Do not let other people's priorities take control of your life.

Balance your actions, and balance your life. Figure 1.2 shows a pie chart representing a sample allocation of the 24 hours in your

GUIDE TO COMMERCIAL PROPERTY CONVERSIONS
SPECIAL 3RD EDITION

day. This shows that you should designate allotted time for the essential activities in your life and strive to maintain that balance.

Identify and control procrastination. Learn to prioritize and focus. There is a good book called "Eat that frog" by Brian Tracy. Do not allow yourself to waste valuable time.

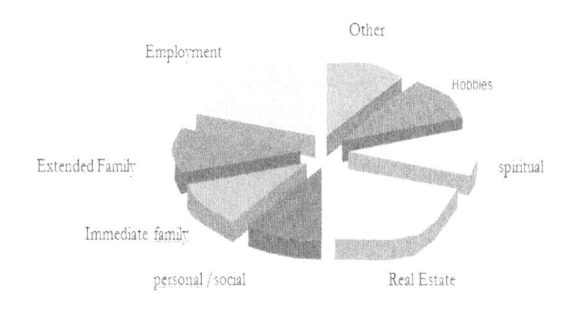

FIGURE 1.2 The pie chart shows that you must allow time for the essential activities of your life. You make your chart like this.

GUIDE TO COMMERCIAL PROPERTY CONVERSIONS
SPECIAL 3RD EDITION

Before we continue

I would like to congratulate you for buying this book and more importantly for starting to read it. Would you believe that 40% of the books that are purchased are never even opened. I often meet people who say they purchased my book a year or so ago but never got round to reading it and then when they did finally read it, they wished that they had done it years ago. So my recommendation here is very simple. Read the book in full and then read it again.

I can't teach you everything and my 17 years' experience in a book in few hours, but I will expand your thinking and help you to recognise how property investing could change your life, which will in turn hopefully inspire you to take action. At the end of the day, it's down to you to take action to achieve the results you desire, but the good news is you don't have to do it on your own because that really can be hard work.

The information that I share in this book is not just theoretical. Although the content is mainly about strategies that work here in the UK, the general principle of finding and helping motivated sellers is a concept that works anywhere in the world, although factors such as financing, taxation and regulations may of course be different in other countries.

CHAPTER 2: WHY TO INVEST IN PROPERTY

"Compounding Result is the 8th wonder of the world"

Traditionally, a pension is simply a form of saving for retirement that has tax benefits. The income paid out to today's pensioners by the state, is funded by those who are working now. As the proportion of people over state pension age grows, the more expensive it gets.

In my opinion, it is unlikely that the state will be able to afford to support us. Probably you would be aware that relying on pension is not going to work. Unless, you do something about it now, which is why I assume you are reading this book.

You have several options for investment, few main ones are:

- ✓ You could invest in shares.
- ✓ You could invest in property.
- ✓ You could start business or similar activities to generate some extra income.

Personally I have done all the above three and I can say this with confidence that investing in property is by far better, simplest and safer.

GUIDE TO COMMERCIAL PROPERTY CONVERSIONS
SPECIAL 3RD EDITION

In case, if you have not started investing until now and feel you will do in near future and this is in your "TO DO" list. Then think twice and read further the benefit of investing earlier than late. Let's first go through more in detail why we should invest and the impact of regular investment or compound. See the table below:

Let's illustrate the tremendous impact of compounding with just one simple but mind-blowing example. Two friends, Yash and John, decide to invest £250 a month. Yash gets started at age 19, keeps going for 10 years and then stops adding to this pot at age 28. In all, he's saved a total of £30,000.

Yash's money then compounds at a rate of 10% a year (10% assumed rate of growth p.a.). By the time he retires at 65, how much does he have? The answer is £1.788 million approx. (see the example spread sheet below). In other words, that modest investment of £30,000 has grown to nearly two million! Pretty stunning, huh?

His friend John gets off to a slower start. He begins investing exactly the same amount £250 a month but doesn't get started

GUIDE TO COMMERCIAL PROPERTY CONVERSIONS
SPECIAL 3RD EDITION

until age 27. Still, he's a disciplined guy, and he keeps investing £250 every month until he's 65 – a period of 39 years. His money also compounds at 10% a year. And the result is? When he retires at 65, he's sitting on a pot of £1.3 million approx.

Let's think about this for a moment. John invested a total of £117,000 almost four times more than the £30,000 that Yash invested. Yet Yash has ended up with an extra £463k. That's right: Yash ends up richer than John, despite the fact that he never invested a penny after the age of 28!

What explains Yash's incredible success? Simple. By starting earlier, the compound interest to be earned on his investment adds more value to his account than he could ever add on his own. By the time he reaches age 52, the compound interest on his account adds over £50,000 per year to his balance. By the time he's 59, his account is growing by more than £100,000 per year! All without adding another penny. John's total return on the money he invested is around 1,000%, whereas Yash's return is a spectacular around 6,000%. This is simply Yash started investing 8 years earlier than John.

GUIDE TO COMMERCIAL PROPERTY CONVERSIONS
SPECIAL 3RD EDITION

That's the awesome power of compounding. Over time this force can turn a modest sum of money into a massive fortune. See full working below:

£250 monthly (£3000 annually) growing at 10% p.a.

Age	Yash	Amount	John	amount
Age 19	£3,000	£3,300		
Age 20	£3,000	£6,930		
Age 21	£3,000	£10,923		
Age 22	£3,000	£15,315		
Age 23	£3,000	£20,147		
Age 24	£3,000	£25,462		
Age 25	£3,000	£31,308		
Age 26	£3,000	£37,738		
Age 27	£3,000	£44,812	£3,000	£3,300
Age 28	£3,000	£52,594	£3,000	£6,930
Age 29		£57,853	£3,000	£10,923
Age 30		£63,638	£3,000	£15,315

GUIDE TO COMMERCIAL PROPERTY CONVERSIONS
SPECIAL 3RD EDITION

Age 31	£70,002	£3,000	£20,147
Age 32	£77,002	£3,000	£25,462
Age 33	£84,702	£3,000	£31,308
Age 34	£93,173	£3,000	£37,738
Age 35	£102,490	£3,000	£ 44,812
Age 36	£112,739	£3,000	£52,594
Age 37	£124,013	£3,000	£61,153
Age 38	£136,414	£3,000	£70,568
Age 39	£150,055	£3,000	£80,925
Age 40	£165,061	£3,000	£92,317
Age 41	£181,567	£3,000	£104,849
Age 42	£199,724	£3,000	£118,634
Age 43	£219,696	£3,000	£133,798
Age 44	£241,666	£3,000	£150,477
Age 45	£265,832	£3,000	£168,825
Age 46	£292,416	£3,000	£189,007
Age 47	£321,657	£3,000	£211.208

GUIDE TO COMMERCIAL PROPERTY CONVERSIONS
SPECIAL 3RD EDITION

Age 48	£353,823	£3,000	£235,629
Age 49	£389,205	£3,000	£262,492
Age 50	£428,126	£3,000	£292,412
Age 51	£470,938	£3,000	£324,545
Age 52	£518,032	£3,000	£360,300
Age 53	£569,835	£3,000	£399,630
Age 54	£626,819	£3,000	£442,893
Age 55	£689,500	£3,000	£490,482
Age 56	£758,451	£3,000	£542,830
Age 57	£834,296	£3,000	£600,413
Age 58	£917,725	£3,000	£663,755
Age 59	£1,009,498	£3,000	£733,430
Age 60	£1,110,447	£3,000	£810,073
Age 61	£1,221,492	£3,000	£894,380
Age 62	£1,343,641	£3,000	£987,118
Age 63	£1,478,00647	£3,000	£1.089,130
Age 64	£1,625,806	£3,000	£1,202,343

GUIDE TO COMMERCIAL PROPERTY CONVERSIONS
SPECIAL 3RD EDITION

| Age 65 | £1,788,387 | £3,000 | £1,324,778 |

| Advantage of investing early: | £463,609 |

But you know what's amazing? Most people never take full advantage of this secret that's lying in full view, this wealth-building miracle that's sitting there right in front of their eyes. Instead, they continue to believe that they can earn their way to become rich. It's a common misperception this belief that, if you earned income is big enough, you'll become financially free.

The truth is, it's not that simple. We've all read stories about movie stars, musicians and athletes who earned more money yet ended up broke because they didn't know how to invest and manage wealth. You may have heard many examples of such people. Even the King of Pop, Michel Jackson, who reportedly signed a recording contract worth almost $1 billion and sold more than 750 million records, supposedly owed more than $300 million upon his death in 2009.

The lesson? You're never going to earn your way to financial freedom. The real route to riches is to set aside a portion of your money and invest it, so that is compounded over many years. That's how you become wealthy while you sleep. That's how you make money work for you instead of you working for money. That's how you achieve true financial freedom. Depending where you invest, your investment can grow even faster than 10% p.a. And good thing is if you invest in property by leveraging well using banks loan and other people money the growths are even faster.

I have been asked many times by people why should we invest in property. And I had explained this why property was such a compelling investment strategy over other asset classes.

So what are some of the reasons why you should invest in property?

GUIDE TO COMMERCIAL PROPERTY CONVERSIONS
SPECIAL 3RD EDITION

Leverage

Leverage is simply utilising debt to finance the acquisition of an asset. In property, one can use leverage not only as a means of increasing the return on equity invested through obtaining a mortgage. This is something that cannot be done with investing in other asset classes e.g. trading stocks and shares or investing money in savings accounts and relying on bank interest. Leverage enables investors invest less money to generate a greater return on investment (ROI). If you go to a bank and ask for £200,000 loan to buy the property more likely, you will get the money funded by the bank as long as everything else is in order such as you have some deposit and good credit etc. Even good thing is if you have not got deposit or good credit you can take this from someone else. And leverage with their money and their credit. However, if you go to a bank and ask for £200,000 loan to invest in stock market, you know the answer, right?

Capital growth

They say property doubles in value every seven to ten years. This isn't necessarily true in all circumstances but property has certainly seen a rise for the last 5-10 years. And if you see the UK house price index or any other countries real estate graphs, you will find the growth is significant. Therefore, a investor's property which initially cost £200,000 in 2012 would now be worth circa £350,000. With a monthly rental income on top of this, it certainly acts as a perpetual advantage to investing in property.

Gearing

Following on from leverage, one facility available to property investors is the ability to 'gear' your portfolio. To explain, this is where one may have £100,000 available and one option is to invest all this money in one property worth £100,000. Alternatively, through gearing, the same £100,000 could be utilized to buy 4 properties at down payment of £25,000 each with 4 buy to let mortgages. This figures I am using for example purpose only, obviously there will be some cost on top and stamp duty etc. but understand this as concept. With the above example in mind, if property prices increase in that area in a year by 25%, should the investor had bought one property for £100,000, his/her property portfolio would now be worth

GUIDE TO COMMERCIAL PROPERTY CONVERSIONS
SPECIAL 3RD EDITION

£125,000. However had the investor used the same equity and invested in four properties their portfolio would now be worth £500,000 (4 x £125,000). Therefore there are great returns to be had in multiple property investment.

Interest rates at an all-time low to date, interest rates are incredibly low and the Bank of England base rate currently sits at 0.25% with more competition in the buy-to-let lenders market than ever, as people buy for a piece of the pie. With servicing mortgage debt being so low, this act as a great opportunity for landlords to re-finance their portfolio, release more equity, purchase additional properties and obtain a greater return.

Tangible/physical asset

Over stocks and shares and other forms of investment, from experience, there is something quite comforting about having an asset that you can touch and feel over something electronic. You know where your property is and know it won't go anywhere! And you can add value to it and control it to a large extend.

GUIDE TO COMMERCIAL PROPERTY CONVERSIONS
SPECIAL 3RD EDITION

Opportunity to add value

There are plenty of opportunities to add value whether it is a refurb project or a lease extension, which are not available in other asset classes. Again using a rough example, you may be able to buy a property which requires some work doing, and increase its value once the works is done. You may struggle to purchase other investments at a reduced price, make them better and resell them for a higher price.

Take away

Impact of compound is like the 8th wonder of the world.

Investment is the only route to make money work for you rather than you work of money.

CHAPTER 3: WHAT IS COMMERCIAL PROPERTY CONVERSION

Any property is generally considered as commercial if it is not residential premises. In other words, A Commercial Property to Residential Conversion, in simple terms, is transforming a commercial property – this is usually an office, pub, care home, or workshop etc – into a residential property, whether it's a block of flats, a HMO or a single dwelling.

One of the benefits that make this investment strategy appealing is that the price of commercial property is generally lower than that of residential properties. This is due to the saturation of the commercial property market.

Another factor that keeps commercial property prices lower than residential ones, is that commercial properties are often left vacant for long periods of times. As a result, the owner is often likely to sell the property quickly, and at a more affordable price, to eradicate their ongoing maintenance costs.

A high percentage of existing commercial properties are located in highly populated and sought after areas – town centres and near key transport links – where there's limited space for new residential properties. If you convert the commercial space into a high quality

GUIDE TO COMMERCIAL PROPERTY CONVERSIONS
SPECIAL 3RD EDITION

residential property, you'll attract a more affluent buyer and be able to let or sell it for a higher premium, which will maximise your ROI.

As you may be aware there is a legislation in UK that allows certain commerical premises to convert into residential without the need of planning permission called permitted development. In May 2013 new rules were introduced by the Department for Communities and Local Government to help developers side step the usual planning processes and use permitted development rights to convert commercial properties into residential.

It was a clear bid to stimulate the market towards increased residential development. The rules give a three year window in which development, provided it does not impact transport the environment or flooding, can press ahead unhindered.

Without question, there is great potential for reusing redundant or inappropriate office accommodation as a way to plug the current housing gap. An estimated 240,000 homes are needed to be built each year for the next few decades to meet demand and control a market that is heating rapidly as the UK accelerates out of recession.

An attractive proposition bearing in mind that VAT has also being recoverable on conversions since rules were changed in the 1990s to try to increase the reuse of vacant properties.

GUIDE TO COMMERCIAL PROPERTY CONVERSIONS
SPECIAL 3RD EDITION

And as Smith and Williamson VAT expert John Voyez pointed out to the seminar, it's a much overlooked issue, but the difference between 20% VAT and 5% of even zero, even in a buoyant market can represent success or failure.

Thus the recent moves to simplify and accelerate the commercial to residential conversion market, would, you might imagine seem rather attractive to developers in a rising post recessionary market with a critical housing shortage.

This *New Rules* gave *New Opportunity* to smart property investor.

GUIDE TO COMMERCIAL PROPERTY CONVERSIONS
SPECIAL 3RD EDITION

CHAPTER 4: WHY DO COMMERCIAL PROPERTY CONVERSION

Why should we use Commercial Property Conversion Investment strategy?

Below are some of my reasons why this strategy is my favourite.

1. It take same time & hassle but better profit, would you like 5 buy to let or 1 Commercial conversion deal?
2. Section 24 of the Finance (no. 2) Act 2015 does not applies to commercial property. this mean section 24 will not affect your investment.
3. Make money by knowing the rules, know the business better than anyone else
4. it can save you lot of time and money
5. it can help you add massive value
6. It may be remove the need for affordable housing
7. it may remove the Local Authority rights to charge of section 106
8. It will seriously save money and time on planning
9. it may mean you can ignore minimum size requirement
10. it may mean section 24 will not affect your investment
11. it may mean less competition comparatively and much more

GUIDE TO COMMERCIAL PROPERTY CONVERSIONS
SPECIAL 3RD EDITION

Six Main Considerations for Commercial to Residential Conversions:

Know your market

Having a strong insight into the current market trends is vital for ensuring that your project yields the return that you want it to. Having a minimum of two but preferably three different exit strategies is very important before you start the project! Will you sell the property once it's completed or will you hold it as a rental property for on-going monthly income and longer-term capital growth? In both cases, pitching the right price is just as important as the conversion itself.

Knowing your market also allows you to approach specialist lenders for funding. However, if you can't show how you will repay their loan, lenders will simply walk away. They want to know 'how much, how long and when does the money come back, with their interest'! They will also need to understand the numbers to see that it's a viable project and that you've covered all the bases and all things stack. Do your research and put a plan in place well before you purchase a property to convert.

Additional Costs

There are many costs involved with Commercial to Residential conversions that you may not yet have considered. You may be

GUIDE TO COMMERCIAL PROPERTY CONVERSIONS
SPECIAL 3RD EDITION

unaware of additional building requirements, such as Part L regulations, which relate to the conversion of fuel and power for your property. Make sure you are fully aware of everything your conversion will require, before committing to the purchase of a commercial property.

Accessibility

Depending on your strategy with the residential property, you will have different requirements. If you are planning to rent your property to families, it will likely be important for them to have vehicle access, which may not be the case if your property is located in a town centre.

External Work

Current legislation makes it easier for investors and developers to convert commercial properties into residential properties. However, this legislation only applies to the interior of the property. Planning permission will likely be required if you intend to alter the exterior of the property. Also, there may be limitations in place, by the local government, as to how you can transform the exterior of the property.

The Surrounding Area

The surroundings of a commercial property may or may not be ideal for a residential property. You'll need to investigate the local

GUIDE TO COMMERCIAL PROPERTY CONVERSIONS
SPECIAL 3RD EDITION

amenities to ensure your tenant/buyer will have access to everything they may need. If the property is in an industrial estate, it will be worth discovering how much the pollution – both environmental and noise – will affect the value and level of attractiveness of your property.

Tax Implications

You will definitely need to consider the VAT treatment of a commercial property purchase, as it will differ from that of a residential property. If you intend to convert the residential property into a commercial one, you should provide the seller with a certificate confirming your conversion plans. However, this could result in the price of the commercial property being increased. Before any action is taken, we urge you to contact property specialist accountant.

Now you may be thinking that it is not easy though. I agree to some extend but once you learn HOW, you can do it easily.

Keep reading this book to learn "HOW"

Let me explain this with an example of small project conversion. Lets say for instance you are involve in a Victorian house conversion into few flats. There will be profit for sure as long as you are doing the things right and profit will depend on the location and type of conversion you are doing. You would more likely be making Tens

GUIDE TO COMMERCIAL PROPERTY CONVERSIONS
SPECIAL 3RD EDITION

of thousands of Pounds rather than Hundreds of thousands of pounds. To get this conversion done, you would more likely be dealing with builder, planning department, make daily decisions, supervise the job, follow up and chase builders, and do so many other things.

On the other hand side, lets say you are involve in a commercial conversion, you might have very similar tasks to do but on a large scale, good thing is here you would be dealing with far better professionals and having all on proper contract with great detailed specification of work. Usually team of professionals here are top of their field. You would be making much more money here for spending your similar time and energy. As an investor we should always focus on Return on investment not just the money invested on the deal but also time invested in a deal.

In my two days of intense workshop, I teach a model called

"D.O L.A.R.G.E ™" in full length.

Let me explain this model more in detail. See chapter six what I mean by **D.O L.A.R.G.E ™**

CHAPTER 5: PRIOR APPROVAL VS FULL PLANNING

"New Law is New opportunity"

Let's first understand the difference between traditional planning method and permitted development. In this book we would give you a balanced perspective on converting commercial buildings, using either the full planning process or the planning shortcut known as prior approval. We and our students mostly uses prior approval as the basis of any deal we do, even if we then go on to add further value by going through an additional process when the opportunity is worthwhile.

Although some investor use prior approval on occasion, they also regularly and successfully goes through a full planning process. However, a full planning process is not to be undertaken lightly as this takes substantial skills and involvement.

FULL PLANNING

What most of the commercial investors agree is that using planning as a means to convert diverse building types into different residential end products combined with taking an uninformed, geographically random approach is likely to lead to a world of pain in the form of frustrated plans, increased costs and excessive delays. One can always choose to do it the hard way if desired or necessary, hut we focus on prior approval

GUIDE TO COMMERCIAL PROPERTY CONVERSIONS
SPECIAL 3RD EDITION

opportunities because the planning system is largely broken. Although gaining planning consent should be policy driven, with policy being written centrally and, in theory, interpreted in the same way throughout the country, the reality is very different. Planning departments are often under-resourced, lacking in experience and driven by the ethos of the Head of Planning, with their decisions often then overseen by untrained and politically motivated councillors, who can be too frequently driven by concerns about where their next vote is coming from.

Let's accept it, you can go and buy all kinds of commercial buildings, such as pubs, offices, care homes , listed buildings or any other commercial building, which don't benefit from prior approval, and you may get planning to convert them and go on to make money. However, if you know there is an easier way, why would you choose to make it difficult for yourself? Both approaches can work, and the great news is that commercial conversions do work, whether you need planning or benefit from prior approval. However, it is certainly true that going through a full planning process seems to be the harder path, especially when you are starting to do commercial property conversion.

Our planning system works like our legal system. The government brings out a new planning policy that is lacking in detail. As with the legal system, nobody knows exactly how to interpret the new planning policy until it is tested, in the first instance by the planning departments, then the planning inspectorate through appeals and then occasionally in the courts. Correct interpretation of each policy is thereby determined by the constant testing of the policy in the context of real applications. Each case determined sets a precedent, and accordingly, the interpretation of each policy should in theory become clearer and clearer, although regrettably some cases seems to serve instead to cloud the issue further! As a result, there is always uncertainty. We also need to remember that this process will be interpreted locally, not nationally. Each local authority might take a different view on planning policy, depending on how it fits with their own agenda, such that they interpret it to fit their own circumstance.

In theory, if you abide by the policies of the planning system, with the help of a good planning consultant who knows the policies themselves as well as the local interpretation of those policies, you should end up getting a green light in the form of a consent. It is a great theory. The problem with it is that it is just that: a theory.

The biggest issue of all seems to be how major decisions on planning issues are made. The local authority hires the planning officers, who are usually trained experts in town planning or other such relevant qualifications, and who will know how to interpret the policies. You, or your planning consultant, then work with the officers to produce a scheme that fulfils their policies by liaising and negotiating with the officers, who again are trained in town planning, and have probably been in the role for years. Having worked together, often for months and after

GUIDE TO COMMERCIAL PROPERTY CONVERSIONS
SPECIAL 3RD EDITION

many iterations involving the production of many reports, we finally get to a point whereby the planning officers recommend the granting of consent. Then what happens? The final decision is handed to untrained, often politically motivated groups of councillors to have their say. Really? Think about this, let a group of experts make a decision based on policy only to then let untrained politicians overturn that decision? If you wrote that down as the basis for a new way of making planning decisions, I believe it would get laughed out of court!

Imagine yourself in that situation. You have gone through the whole costly and time-consuming process, and you then find yourself standing before a bunch of often politically-motivated, untrained town planning amateurs who overturn the decision, thereby volunteering you for either abortive costs, further months of work, further design costs and/or additional reports, or possibly even an additional timely and costly planning appeal. And they wonder why more houses are not being built by smaller developers?

Even once you receive your planning consent, you will then often have to enter into a Section 106 Agreement negotiation, although this may sometimes be done in parallel with the application itself. A Section 106 Agreement is a legal agreement whereby the developer is required to pay a contribution towards any number of local needs as laid out in local policy, to include funding towards schools, hospitals, roads, surgeries, green space and much more. It can take many months to negotiate. Furthermore, It is a legal agreement that needs negotiating between sets

GUIDE TO COMMERCIAL PROPERTY CONVERSIONS
SPECIAL 3RD EDITION

of lawyers representing both the council and the developer. And who do you think pays all the legal bills, including those of the local authority?

When different departments of the local authority argue amongst themselves about what their priorities are, they are arguing with each other on your legal bill. Currently, you may also get a Community Infrastructure Levy (CIL) thrown into the mix. I seem to recall that CIL was brought in to eventually remove the need for a Section 106, and to make negotiations much simpler by coming up with a simple tariff that developers could look at and know very quickly what they were going to have to pay. A worthy goal indeed. Instead, what seems to happen in most areas is that we now have BOTH Section 106 Agreements to negotiate and CIL payments to make too!

A full planning process can take months, and it can cost a considerable amount of money. One example is reports. The local authority will often ask you to come up with different reports to cover various areas of concern. Many of these reports, and the need for them, are completely legitimate and entirely justified. For instance, ensuring that a site hasn't been contaminated in a way rendering it unfit for human habitation would seem essential. However, the problem is that local authorities are so worried about being found liable for making bad decisions that they will often cover their risk by asking developers to come up with what seems like every report conceivable, just in case they come up with something material. Some of these reports appear to be almost completely unnecessary.

Given all this negativity surrounding the risks of using a full planning process in your development journey, unless you are an expert in it, it's very difficult to make it work for you - an expert for your chosen conversion type in your selected locality. You need to instruct a really good planning consultant and stay in one area, where you get to know what they prioritise, what they like and what they don't like. And, even if you do that, you need to steel yourself for a lot of hard work and possible extra costs. Of course, that presents a problem because investors don't like unknown timescales. Worse, they are extremely nervous about unknown costs with an unknown outcome. So, even if you want to use planning, you then need to find investors who are comfortable with the associated risks.

Prior Approval

Contrast that approach with the government- sanctioned planning shortcut that is called prior approval.

Before we start to excite too many of you, we must state that prior approval rules have at the time of writing only been applied in England, and accordingly, Scotland, Wales and Northern Ireland do not benefit from these rights. Furthermore, a limited number of areas in England have secured exemption from prior approval. These are listed in the government prior approval document available via the links provided later in this book.

GUIDE TO COMMERCIAL PROPERTY CONVERSIONS
SPECIAL 3RD EDITION

For those fortunate enough to live or operate in England, prior approval is essentially a pre-determined permission to convert some buildings in specified commercial use classes to residential use, more specifically C3 residential use (essentially for people living together as single household). There are specified conditions to be met for each prior approval class, but as long as those conditions are met, planning approval will be forthcoming. Commonly, the basic conditions of flood, highways, contamination and noise must be checked, with some classes having further tests to be undertaken. Furthermore, prior approval applications are required to be determined within 56 days - just eight weeks - at a fixed cost of only £80, no matter how large the application. Although prior approval applications are generally determined in 56 days, there have been occasions cropping up more recently where the incredibly stretched planning departments are requesting extensions of time, usually small, but generally speaking the timetable is still relatively certain.

Should you find that a building fails one of the tests laid out in the criteria, this does not render prior approval unobtainable. Instead, one merely needs to determine the mitigation required to bring the results of the test back to an acceptable result. For example, if a site was found to be contaminated, then the applicant would simply have to agree with a suitably qualified person what works would be required to bring the site to an acceptably 'uncontaminated' level suitable for residential use. By submitting that remediation plan with the prior approval application, the

GUIDE TO COMMERCIAL PROPERTY CONVERSIONS
SPECIAL 3RD EDITION

local authority should then issue the prior approval with a condition requiring the suggested works are carried out, and that evidence is collated thereafter to confirm that in so doing, the land had been rendered acceptably 'clean'.

The list of use classes benefitting from these rights is constantly changing, but at the time of writing, prior approval exists for B1 a offices, A1 and A2 retail, B8 storage (soon to finish), B1c light industrial, agricultural buildings, and some sui generis uses, such launderettes, arcades and casinos. It is possible that they will extend this to other use classes, but at present we don't know what they are going to be.

More recently, some local authorities in England have started to apply for Article 4 exemptions from some prior approval rights, usually the prior approval pertaining to the conversion of offices. Accordingly, it's always worth checking the latest status of prior approval in your area with a good planning consultant.

Benefit of prior Approval

- The prior approval has a fixed fee of £80, no matter how big the scheme being applied for. If one is undertaking a larger scheme of say 50-60 apartments under normal planning process, that could cost you tens of thousands of pounds as a planning fee. However, by using prior approval, the fixed fee for any size remains £80.

GUIDE TO COMMERCIAL PROPERTY CONVERSIONS
SPECIAL 3RD EDITION

- Prior approval applications should be determined within 56 days.

- Prior approval applications can only be failed in pre-determined circumstances:

    - Unresolved issues with any of the four following tests: flooding,
    highways, contamination and noise from neighbouring!

    - Prior approval does not apply to any listed building, regardless of where it is located or whether it is Grade I or Grade II

    - CA conservation area for some building classes

    - Sites of special scientific interest (SSSI) for some building classes

    - AONB area of outstanding natural beauty for some building classes

To understand this more, it doesn't matter if an office is in a conservation area, or an SSSI or even an AONB. To understand this, we need to consider the principle of prior approval. Prior approval is for changing the internal use of the building. You are not allowed to make external changes without an additional planning application, unless it is explicitly allowed within the rules of the prior approval guidelines, as it is, for example shops.

Prior approval also removes any minimum size requirements, more

GUIDE TO COMMERCIAL PROPERTY CONVERSIONS
SPECIAL 3RD EDITION

specifically Nationally Described Space Standards. We will describe the real impact of this in the redesign section of the book, but at this point let's just acknowledge the extra flexibility of the freedom to determine the sizes of the residential units we are seeking to create. A word of caution, even at this early stage: if you are intending to sell the units at any stage, mortgage lenders will not generally lend on any unit of less than 30 sq. m. of internal space.

Prior approval conversions also benefit from being exempt from affordable housing requirements - again, however large the scheme is. This is an extraordinary benefit, particularly as one starts to take on bigger schemes for which, if using a traditional full planning process, local authorities may be looking for very significant contributions. Such contributions could be financial payments or actual units, and can exceed of 35% or more of the development.

With regard to the highways test, given that most commercial buildings will be in or near towns and cities, it is usually possible to demonstrate a sustainable transport plan to include bus routes, trains, parking, either on-site or locally and cycle stores on top of amenities within walking distance. So highways is often a non-issue for many developments, but you need to bear in mind what it might be for your chosen niches. The key issue is being able to provide some sort of sustainable transport plan, and again, your planning consultant should be able to guide you on that very early in the process.

GUIDE TO COMMERCIAL PROPERTY CONVERSIONS
SPECIAL 3RD EDITION

Checking for contamination is usually commenced by getting a desktop survey done. The desktop survey will tell you if there are any likely contamination "Issues; if there are, then the consultant who undertakes the survey should work with the planning consultant to agree what further reports and/or mitigation are required. As long as that is covered in the prior approval application, it should suffice.

Checking for flood risk is also initially a desktop survey. The process is almost exactly the same as for contamination, though mitigation is somewhat different and covered in the redesign section.

To summarise, overall benefit of prior approval, it allows us to give greater certainty, for ourselves and our investors, because it is permission driven by legislation rather than by committee.

Using prior approval means:

- you know you'll get permission
- you know how long the process will take
- you avoid affordable housing requirements
- there are no minimum size requirements
- there is usually no requirement for Section 106, unless specific issues arise
- you can't be failed for lack of parking in a town centre, as long as you can demonstrate a sustainable transport plan (local amenities, bus

routes, trains, bikes etc.)

These are all very important in your pitch to your investor, as they ensure:

- certain outcome
- certain timeline
- no unexpected costs for affordable housing or Section 106 (normally)
- maximum return on investment
- The full government PD Order can be found at: http://www.legislation.gov.uk/uksi/2015/596/contents/made
- There was an update to this document in May 2016, which can be found here: http://www.legislation.go.uk/uksi/2016/332/made

Once your planning consultant has completed and submitted your prior approval application and you demonstrate mitigation for any test failures, you should receive your response within 56 days, and your response will be one of only three outcomes:

- Prior Approval Not Required
- Prior Approval Required and Granted
- Prior Approval Required but Not Granted

The first response is the confusing one - prior approval not required. Does that sound like a green light? No, I didn't think so either, but that is the green light. It seems to mean say you don't need approval, but that is the government's way of saying you have got it! that is your green light.

The second one Prior Approval Required and Granted – is a conditional approval.

If you needed to provide mitigation for one of the Tests (a flooding for example), you then submitted your suggested mitigation for that test with your application and if the local authority was happy with mitigation suggestion, they accordingly grant you prior approval. The second response says prior approval is required because you did identify some issues, but they are happy with what you suggested.

The third one, you do not want to get; prior approval is required because you have identified some issues but they are not happy with the mitigation you suggested and it is therefore not granted. You shouldn't ever see this result, as your planning consultant shouldn't let you get to this stage. They should be in dialogue with the local authority and make sure the mitigation you suggested will be acceptable, and if they want different or further mitigation, it should be negotiated while the application is live. Although you shouldn't see this result, but don't panic if you do. It is not the end of the story. You or your planning consultant needs to go and chat with the local authority, and figure out what exactly they are looking for.

CHAPTER 6: NEW PERMITTED DEVELOPMENT LAW 2020

You can perform certain types of work without needing to apply for planning permission. These are called "permitted development rights"

They derive from a general planning permission granted not by the local authority but by Parliament. Bear in mind that the permitted development rights, which apply, to many common projects for houses do not apply to flats, maisonettes or other buildings. Similarly, commercial properties have different permitted development rights to dwellings.

In some areas of the country, known generally as 'designated areas', permitted development rights are more restricted. For example, if you live in:

- a Conservation Area
- a National Park
- an Area of Outstanding Natural Beauty
- a World Heritage Site or
- the Norfolk or Suffolk Broads.

GUIDE TO COMMERCIAL PROPERTY CONVERSIONS
SPECIAL 3RD EDITION

You will need to apply for planning permission for certain types of work which do not need an application in other areas. There are also different requirements if the property is a listed building.

The Planning Portal's general advice is that you should contact your local planning authority and discuss your proposal before any work begins. They will be able to inform you of any reason why the development may not be permitted and if you need to apply for planning permission for all or part of the work.

A planning consultant may help with the smooth running of your project and guide you on your permitted development requirements.

...

Permitted Development Rights withdrawn

You should also note that the local planning authority may have removed some of your permitted development rights by issuing an 'Article 4' direction. This will mean that you have to submit a planning application for work which normally does not need one.

Article 4 directions are made when the character of an area of acknowledged importance would be threatened. They are most common in conservation areas. You will probably know if your property is affected by such a direction, but you can check with the local planning authority if you are not sure.

GUIDE TO COMMERCIAL PROPERTY CONVERSIONS
SPECIAL 3RD EDITION

Please note: Houses created through permitted development rights to change use from shops, financial and professional services premises or agricultural buildings cannot use householder permitted development rights to improve, alter or extend homes: planning permission is required. You are advised to contact your local planning authority.

Legislation

The Town and Country Planning (General Permitted Development) (England) Order 2015 is the principal order.

The Order sets out classes of development for which a grant of planning permission is automatically given, provided that no restrictive condition is attached or that the development is exempt from the permitted development rights.

What are the new permitted development rules?

What is the **new** right? From 31 August 2020, a **new permitted development** right will allow you to construct up to two additional storeys to dwelling houses consisting of at least two storeys, and one additional storey to one storey dwelling houses. The **new** storeys must be immediately above the topmost storey.

GUIDE TO COMMERCIAL PROPERTY CONVERSIONS
SPECIAL 3RD EDITION

The Government has now implemented significant changes to the use classes system in England (Use Class Order 1987) through the new Town and Country Planning (Use Classes) (Amendment) (England) Regulations 2020. The main driver of change has been a need to enable the repurposing of buildings on high street and town centres.

The Regulations contain some detailed transitional provisions which will affect how and when changes take effect in practice. The Regulations came into force on **1 September 2020**. Separately, the Government has announced major changes to the permitted development regime.

Use Classes

The Regulations introduce three new use classes (E, F1 and F2). The most significant change is the creation of a new "Commercial, Business and Service" use called "Class E". This brackets together a wide variety of uses, all of which are now considered to be in the same use class:

- Retail
- Restaurants
- Financial, professional or other commercial services
- Publicly accessible indoor sport, recreation or fitness

GUIDE TO COMMERCIAL PROPERTY CONVERSIONS
SPECIAL 3RD EDITION

- Publicly available medical or health services
- Crèches, day nurseries and day centres
- Offices, including research and development
- Industrial uses which do not harm amenity.

Planning permission is not required for changes of use within the same use class. This means that many types of business user will be able to change the uses of properties without seeking planning permission. For example, under the new rules, a shop will be able to change to an office and then to a gym and back again, without planning permission.

The residential (C classes), general industrial (B2) and storage and distribution (B8) use classes remain unchanged, except for a new cross-reference in the B2 class to the new Class E.

Some of the community type uses have been put together in the new Class F1 and Class F2. Class F1 refers to learning and non-residential institutions where there is generally wider public use such as school, libraries and art galleries. Class F2 refers to local community facilities where classes groups together such as community halls and meeting spaces, uses which provide for physical group activities such as swimming pools, skating rinks and areas for outdoor sports and a small, local shop like one you would find in a rural community or a large residential development.

GUIDE TO COMMERCIAL PROPERTY CONVERSIONS
SPECIAL 3RD EDITION

A further significant change is the confirmation of a new list of *sui generis* uses. *Sui generis* uses generally cannot be changed to any other use without planning permission. The new list of *sui generis* uses includes:

- Pubs, wine bars and other drinking establishments (including those with expanded food provision)
- Hot food takeaways
- Live music venues
- Cinemas, concert halls, bingo halls and dance halls.

Practical consequences

From 1 September 2020 to 31 July 2021, permitted development rights enabling a change of use will continue to be applied based on the existing use classes, as they existed on 31 August 2020. For example, the office to residential permitted development right will continue to have effect pursuant to the existing system.

Planning applications submitted before 1 September 2020 that cite the current use classes must continue to be decided by the local planning authority using the former uses classes after 1 September 2020, so there will be no change there.

In order to change the uses within a class, there must have been actual and lawful use (i.e. if the building is not being used or occupied for the use permitted under an existing planning permission, it will need to be bought into that use before it can then change to another use within Class E).

Permitted development rights

The Government has also implemented, in parallel, a separate series of changes to permitted development rights. In summary, the following additional permitted development rights are available:

- From 31 August 2020, there will be a new permitted development right allowing the demolition and rebuilding of "vacant and redundant" office and light industrial buildings into dwellings, without planning permission.

- From 31 August 2020, new permitted development rights will enable the upward extension, by up to two storeys, of existing postwar-built homes. These rights will also be extended to the creation of new homes above terraces, offices and shops, without planning permission.

Both rights will require that prior approval is sought from the local authority prior to commencement of the development. This includes approval in respect of traffic and highway matters, air traffic and defence asset impacts, contamination risks, flood risk, the external appearance of the building, the provision of adequate natural light in all habitable rooms of the new dwellings, impact on amenity of the existing building and neighbouring premises including overlooking, privacy and loss of light, and the impact on any protected views.

The key constraint is that the upward extension rights will only apply to existing residential dwellings or purpose-built, detached blocks of flats. Mixed-use buildings will not benefit from these new rights.

Potential legal challenge

At the current time, a pre-action protocol letter has been submitted to the Ministry for Housing, Communities and Local Government in respect of both the changes to the use classes order and the new permitted development rights. The letter alleges a failure to meaningfully consider consultation responses, breach of the Public Sector Equality Duty and failure to carry out an appropriate Environmental Impact Assessment. The Government was required to reply by 26 August 2020, or else the applicant has threatened to seek interim relief as part of a judicial review application, preventing these legal provisions from having effect.

Effect of changes

Permitted development

The new permitted development rights significantly extend the scope of new development which can be carried out without planning permission. The process of prior approval will have the effect of mitigating some of the most harmful impacts of those developments, but the major practical consequence is that infrastructure contributions can only be sought in relation to the matters approved through the prior approval process. Government-commissioned research also indicates that converted dwellings built using permitted development rights are generally significantly worse, in terms of every qualitative metric, than equivalent dwellings with planning permission.

Use classes

The new use classes will also have secondary impacts on other processes which are informed by the use class regime (i.e. valuation procedures, which will have to account for a wider range of possible uses, and statutory nuisance, because changing uses can result in additional amenity impacts). For those local authorities with policies which seek to protect town centre uses or office uses in particular locations, the changes will undermine those policies by allowing developers to sidestep those parts of the planning regime entirely.

Conclusion

Taken together, the changes represent a very significant shift in control away from local authorities and the communities they represent, into a significantly less regulated environment.

GUIDE TO COMMERCIAL PROPERTY CONVERSIONS
SPECIAL 3RD EDITION

Overall, local planning authorities will lose a significant degree of control over changes of use, and may seek alternative routes to manage changes of use (including imposing more restrictive planning conditions, or the use of Article 4 directions). There is a silver lining for authorities in this respect, in that the changes may result in increased take-up of otherwise disused units, which in turn may have a beneficial impact in terms of business rates.

In addition, the changes are very significant, but are only the tip of the iceberg for potential planning changes on the immediate horizon. The Government's current White Paper foreshadows the possibility of swinging changes to the entire planning system over the coming months, including the potential implementation of a consolidated infrastructure levy, and it may well be that further permitted development reforms follow in kind.

Summary of New PD Rights:

New PD rights - From September 2020

- **Class AA** – New Flats on detached Commercial or Mixed use buildings (Shop & 2 upper floors)

- **Class AB** - New Flats terraced mixed use building (2 storeys)

- **Class AC** – New Flats on Terraced Houses

GUIDE TO COMMERCIAL PROPERTY CONVERSIONS
SPECIAL 3RD EDITION

- **Class ZA** – Demolition and Rebuild of Offices or Light Industrial unit

Advantages of this New Rules:

- This offers a lot of scope with some restrictions
- Allows property developers to do many things which, no doubt, will be reviewed in the future.
- Quick Action takers will WIN

New Commercial Usage E Class - From September 2020

- Old A1 – Shops, Retail Warehouses, Off-licences, dry cleaners, post office etc
- Old A2 – Banks, Building Societies, Betting Shops, estate agents etc.
- Old A3 – Café & Restaurants
- Old B1 – Offices
- Some of Old D1 (Non – residential) – Health Centres, clinic, day nurseries
- Some of Old D2 – Gym, indoor recreations

GUIDE TO COMMERCIAL PROPERTY CONVERSIONS
SPECIAL 3RD EDITION

New E Class - From September 2020

New E Class – From Sep 2020

- **New Commercial Usage Class E**
  Expires 31st Jul 2021
  - Old A1 – Retail shops
  - Old A2 – Banks, travel agents, estate agents
  - Old A3 – Restaurants
  - Old B1 – Offices

  → CLASS G
  → CLASS M
  → CLASS O

Exiting PD rights – Expires 31st July 2021

- **Class O** – Office to residential Conversion into multiples flats
- **Class M** – Flats at rear of ground floor retail unit
- **Class G** – 2 Flats above a retail unit

Advantages of this Existing Rules:

- No Minimum Space standard at present (from 6th April 2021 – Minimum 37 sqm required)
- Class G and O can be done in Conservation areas
- Deemed Consent after 56 days for Class M & O (Class G required no prior consent)
- This will be replaced by new PD rules

GUIDE TO COMMERCIAL PROPERTY CONVERSIONS
SPECIAL 3RD EDITION

In the next section I am going to explore little more about one of my favourite strategy "Commerical Property Conversion".

CHAPTER 7: COMMERCIAL PROPERTY CONVERSION MODEL

There are various property investments strategies that I teach in my 3 days Master Class workshop. There is also two days workshop I run mainly to focus commerical conversion strategy in detail.

In this section I am going to explore little more about one of my favourite strategy "Commerical Property Conversion".

Let me explain this model more in detail. See below what I mean by **L.A.R.G.E ™**

L – Locate commerical Property deals

A – Arrange Funds

R – Redesign

G – Get it built

E – Exit Plan

DO – stand for Delegate and Outsource

Lets go little more deeper to understand this model.

L – Locate commerical Property deals

GUIDE TO COMMERCIAL PROPERTY CONVERSIONS
SPECIAL 3RD EDITION

You can locate the commercial property deals through various sources, In addition to the other ways I explained in this book earlier below are other sources where you can locate the commerical property deals for commercial conversion.

1. Property Estate gazette https://propertylink.estatesgazette.com/
2. Rightmove http://www.rightmove.co.uk
3. Zoopla https://www.zoopla.co.uk/
4. Commercial agents (local agents and national agents like JLL, Savills, Knigh Frank, CBRE, DTZ, LSH, GVA, Cluttons, Cushman wakefield, Colliers etc)
5. Fleurets https://www.fleurets.com/
6. CoStar Shopproperty http://www.shopproperty.co.uk/
7. Commercial and residential Auctions
8. Brewery companies
9. Land Agents
10. Network Events

A – Arrange Funds

You would need to arrange funds. Normally traditional loans are not ideal for this type of deals. So you would need a property commercial mortgage broker. You may need to arrange bridging finance or have JV partner and High net worth Individuals (HNWI funds. Unfortunately I am unable to explain all about how to arrange the funds in this book. I run a separate one-day workshop to teach how to raise funds and get Joint venture partners. However you can download free Joint Venture elevator pitch from my website at www.propertyexpertsacademy.com under freebies section.

R – Redesign

As you may be able to see in order to add value we need to redesign the building, the more creative you are here higher profit you will make. Do not just rely on the architect here unless they think as an investor and know what would fetch the maximum value and will be more appealing to sell fast. Also don't just see the empty shell of the buildings, think beyond, many properties have huge garden or car park area that could attract great development opportunities. I usually cover this more in details in my 2 days Commercial Property Conversion workshop. Having said that if you are really keen to progress and cannot attend my workshop for some reason just drop me an email and I would be happy to work with right people on project to project basis.

G – Get it built

Getting the building work done property is very important. You should have the right time and right system in place to execute the building process. But not to worry as you can get professional and team to do the work for you. You can hire project manager to manage the property for you at set percentage of contract value for Project manage.

GUIDE TO COMMERCIAL PROPERTY CONVERSIONS
SPECIAL 3RD EDITION

E – Exit Plan

You can plan your exit strategy whether you like cash flow and retain the property or sell the units to make profit or do bit of both. You need to bear in mind the tax implications, so you should plan your exit strategy in such a way that leave most of the profit in your pocket rather than paying to Tax Man. You should hire the right tax consultant to advise you.

VAT in connection with converting a commercial property for residential use is a complex area. It is important to get it right so as to avoid any nasty surprises and to reduce the construction costs associated with the project.

Generally, if work is carried out to an existing building, VAT would be chargeable at the standard rate of 20%.

However, the reduced VAT rate of 5% could be applied in certain circumstances, for example where there is a conversion of a commercial building into a residential dwelling.

i.e. If an office building is converted into a residential building at a net cost of £500,000, the difference in the VAT rates could be worth £75,000.

The reduced rate applies to: Conversion of a non-residential building such as a barn or warehouse into dwellings; Conversions involving a change in the number of dwellings within the building i.e.

conversion of a house which creates additional dwellings or conversion of multiple occupancy dwellings into one house; Or the renovation of residential property that has been unoccupied for more than 2 years.

The main condition for the reduced rate is that there cannot be any planning restrictions on the building that will prevent the property from being sold or used separately from any other land or building (note occupancy restrictions do not prevent separate use or disposal). An example of this restriction could be a barn that can only be sold or used along with the nearby farmhouse.

The reduced rate will cover costs relating to fabrics of the buildings such as walls, roof, floors, stairs, doors, windows, plumbing and wiring; Provision of facilities such as water, power, heat and drainage; Installation of sanitary-ware, central heating, light fittings and fitted kitchen units.

Costs relating to services such as architects and quantity surveyors, the installation of goods that are not building materials (such as carpets or fitted bathroom furniture) or costs relating to the hire of goods or scaffolding remain chargeable to VAT at the standard rate. If the builder undertakes the work and purchases materials on the owner's behalf, they should only charge VAT at 5% on both labour and materials.

GUIDE TO COMMERCIAL PROPERTY CONVERSIONS
SPECIAL 3RD EDITION

VAT Pitfalls for converting a Commercial premises to Residential use

Where the builder incorrectly charges VAT at the standard rate rather than the reduced rate, HMRC will not pay the excess back. In such cases, it would be up to the owner to recover the money back from the builders, so it is imperative that the tax treatment is considered upfront to ensure the correct amount of VAT is paid.

DO – stand for Delegate and Outsource

See below simple calculation to show as example:

Commercial Conversion Example

	Amount
Bought a Commercial building around 7000 sq. feet	£600,000
Used bank loan @5% to get 75% LTV	£450,000

GUIDE TO COMMERCIAL PROPERTY CONVERSIONS
SPECIAL 3RD EDITION

Joint venture funds used to purchase	£150,000
Joint venture funds used to convert the building in to 10 flats	£700,000
Sold 10 flats	£2,500,000
Profit made (250000-£600000-£700000-£30,000 interest)	£1,170,000
Profit split with JV partner 50:50	£585,000

For JV partner making £585,000 extra on his investment of £850000 was great over a period of 12 to 18 months. This example is just to give you an idea about what sort of return you can make, obviously you got to consider few other bits such as while property is empty you may require to pay some business rates, stamp duty at purchase etc that we have not factored into this example to keep the calculation easy to understand.

Another good thing is you can either hire professionals to do these tasks or outsource the whole construction project. You can even sell the deal after packaging it for a good profit or work in joint venture with someone who can come up with other skills and value.

I would also highly recommend to go through more about the legislation by using the below links

http://www.legislation.gov.uk/uksi/2015/596/made

http://www.legislation.gov.uk/uksi/2016/332/made

You also need to be aware of VAT 1614d, CPSE's, Drafts Contracts, lease surrender, lease re-grant and Heads of Terms etc

I believe you would agree with me that you would need more time to research on this area and prepare yourself before choosing this strategy. Alternatively, you can join my 2 days' workshop to learn all about Commercial Property Conversion practically step by step and join the team to take regular benefits.

GUIDE TO COMMERCIAL PROPERTY CONVERSIONS
SPECIAL 3RD EDITION

What you will take away from the 2 days' Commercial Conversion workshop

1. Step-by-step guide how to identify property and offer and deal with conveyancing
2. How to source a deal under your competitor's nose
3. 6 common mistakes to avoid
4. Planning shortcut to bigger profit with less risk
5. Creatively splitting the titles and adding £10,000s

CHAPTER 8: CONSTRUCTION PROJECT MANAGEMENT ESSENTIALS

"Well Plan is half done"

Construction Project management is the whole training on its own. However we are not trying to teach you here how to become project management but it is important to understand the basic about project managers role while you are dealing with commerical property conversion.

Skills of project manager

<u>Technical</u>

Contract practice

Managing people

Procurement and tendering

Programming and planning

Construction

Leadership

GUIDE TO COMMERCIAL PROPERTY CONVERSIONS
SPECIAL 3RD EDITION

Project administration

Project process and procedures

Risk management

Commercial management of construction

Development appraisals

Development/project briefs

Project audit

Project evaluation

Professional

Being ethical

Client care

Communication and negotiation

Health and safety

Accounting principles and procedures

Business planning

Conflict avoidance, management and dispute

resolution procedures

Data management

Sustainability

GUIDE TO COMMERCIAL PROPERTY CONVERSIONS
SPECIAL 3RD EDITION

Team working

Managing resources

Key stage of project

RIBA Work Stages	CoP for Project Management for Construction and Development
0 Strategy	Inception
1 Brief	Feasibility
2 Concept Design	Strategy
3 Developed Design	Pre-construction
4 Technical Design	Construction
5 Construction	Engineering Services & Commissioning
6 Hand Over	Completion, Handover & Occupation
7 Use	Post-Completion Review/Close out Report

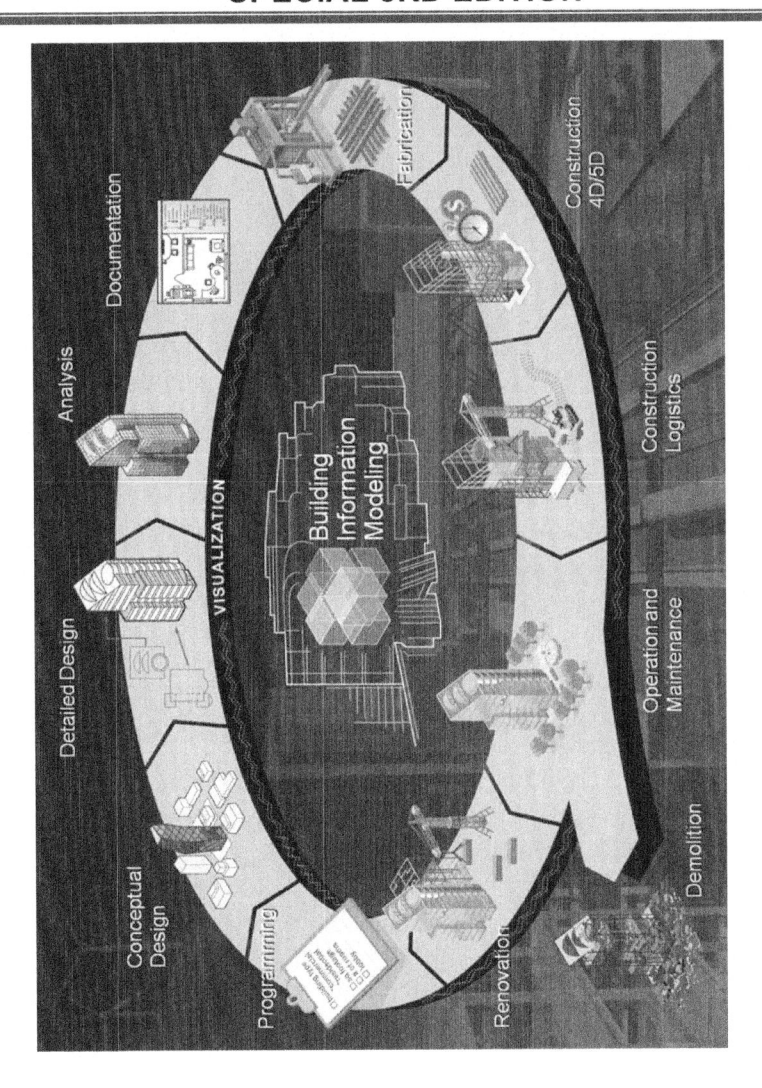

GUIDE TO COMMERCIAL PROPERTY CONVERSIONS
SPECIAL 3RD EDITION

Example of project various stages

GUIDE TO COMMERCIAL PROPERTY CONVERSIONS
SPECIAL 3RD EDITION

Team Roles:

- Sponsor (Client, Funder)
- PM
- Quantity Surveyor (Pre and Post)
- Architect
- Mechanical Engineer
- Electrical Engineer
- Structural Engineer
- Civils Engineer
- Finance (accountant)
- Solicitor
- Acoustician
- Clerk of Works
- Catering
- Theatre
- Business Planner
- Landscape Architect
- Etc etc

GUIDE TO COMMERCIAL PROPERTY CONVERSIONS
SPECIAL 3RD EDITION

Example of various professionals and contractor in project.

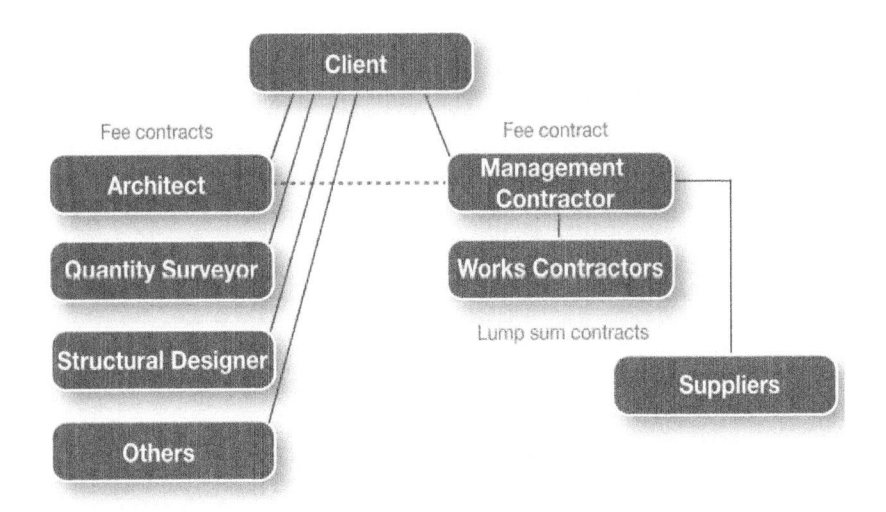

```
                    ┌────────┐
                    │ Client │
                    └────────┘
    Fee contracts              Fee contract
   ┌───────────┐            ┌──────────────┐
   │ Architect │------------│  Management  │
   └───────────┘            │  Contractor  │
                            └──────────────┘
   ┌──────────────────┐     ┌──────────────┐
   │ Quantity Surveyor│     │Works Contractors│
   └──────────────────┘     └──────────────┘
                              Lump sum contracts
   ┌──────────────────┐            ┌───────────┐
   │Structural Designer│           │ Suppliers │
   └──────────────────┘            └───────────┘
   ┌────────┐
   │ Others │
   └────────┘
```

Legislation

What legislation or laws must a Project Manager be aware of in the construction / development industry?

Legislation

- Planning
- Building Regulations
- Health & Safety
- Environmental Legislation
- Property Laws
- Contract Laws
- Others (Highways, Money Laundering, Bribery etc)

Funding & Finance

- Capital
- Revenue
- Banks
- Mezzanine Finance
- Grants
- Cash Flows
- Valuations
- Development Appraisals

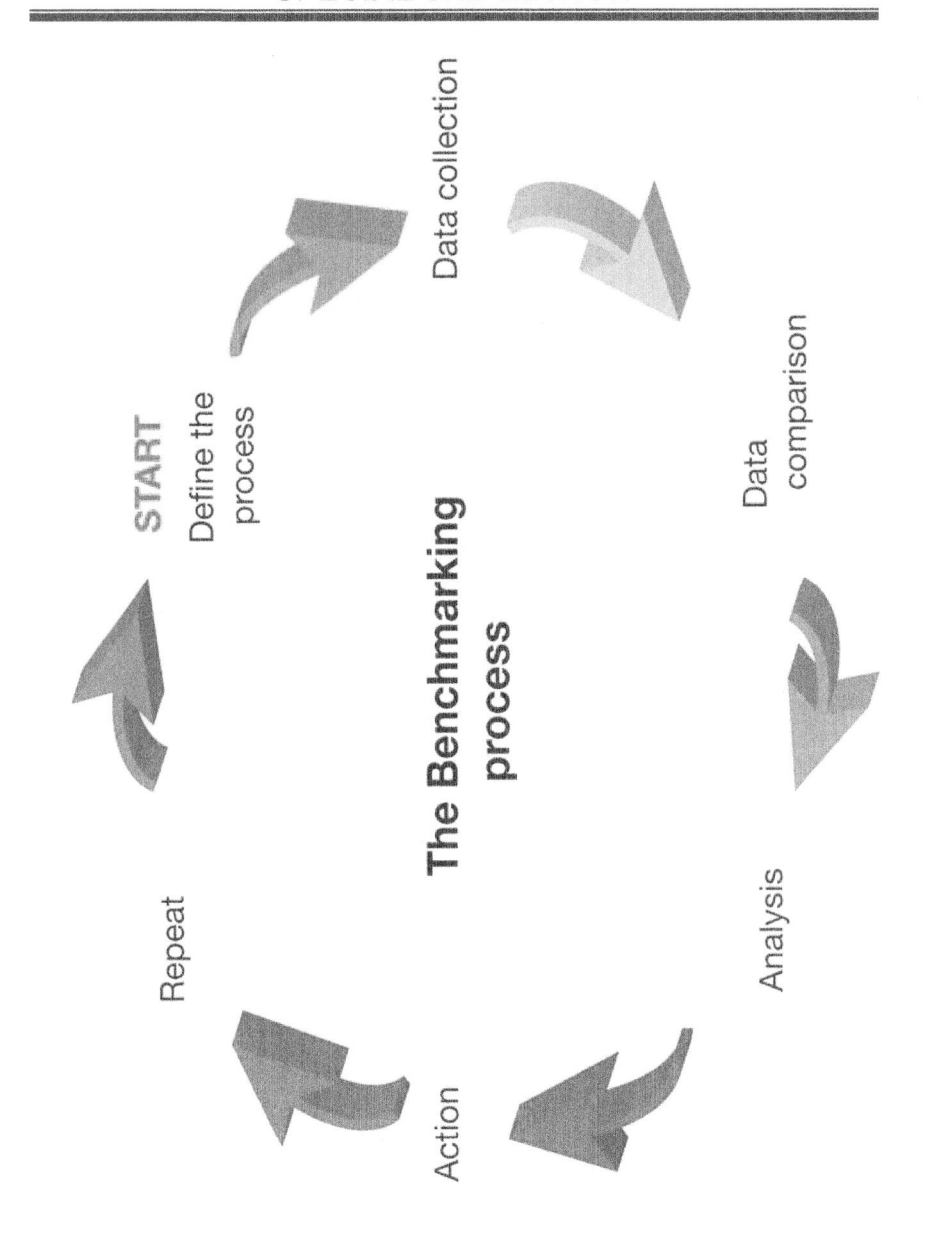

GUIDE TO COMMERCIAL PROPERTY CONVERSIONS
SPECIAL 3RD EDITION

The Benchmarking process

- START — Define the process
- Data collection
- Data comparison
- Analysis
- Action
- Repeat

CHAPTER 9: TITLE SPLITTING AND CREATING LEASES

"Be creative and add value without even physically touching the property"

Creating the leases and the clauses go in it can create additional profit. Let me explain this to you with an example of box of 10 beer. Say a guy goes to supermarket and buys a box of 10 beers and sell them individually. It is same in property field. Say if you buy box of 10 beers for £700,000 and sales them individually for £100,000 each so what's the profit? If your answer is £300,000 then it's wrong. You probably has missed the Cardboard container value. The cardboard container is the freehold title here. The cardboard container is worth something. We will discuss later about how to find the intrinsic value of freeholder (the value of cardboard box).

Let me first explain what benefit someone would have who own the freehold or would plan to buy such freehold.

1. Lease extension value (reversionary value)
2. possession (at the end of the lease terms)
3. Ground Rent (Regular Rental Income)
4. Management (fees for managing the block/property communal area)

GUIDE TO COMMERCIAL PROPERTY CONVERSIONS
SPECIAL 3RD EDITION

5. Building insurance (commission on annual premium)

6. Freehold intrinsic value& hope value (future development potential)

When you buy a leasehold flat you are not buying that flat but you are buying a piece of paper / lease that allows you to occupy that flat for a long period of time on a certain terms. Typical long leases would be like 99 years or 125 years etc. You can read more about this under the Leasehold Reform, housing and urban development Act 1993 (as amended by commonhold and leasehold Reform ACT 2002.

When you have freehold you have some hope value. Say leaseholder can not do loft extension without freeholder's consent. Normally every landlord/freeholder would allow leasehold consent provided leaseholder can pay a reasonable money to freeholder in return. You might say but that is in future why we value now. Here is the thing, if you sell that freehold to someone, people in the market would be prepare to pay a money for that hope value / future potential.

If you are a large institutional investor who own various freehold buildings that every week somewhere or the other leaseholder would require lease extension, some would require licence of alternation, deed of variation, consent to assign the lease etc for which freeholder would charge some money. That's how your freehold gets value for its freehold title.

GUIDE TO COMMERCIAL PROPERTY CONVERSIONS
SPECIAL 3RD EDITION

Various clauses in the lease would add values in the freehold, however at the same time you got to balance by not making the lease completely favourable to freehold or it would be difficult to sell the leaseholder flat. for example if you are cutting the cake into the slices and selling the slice individually that slice should take good. It need to have some icing / cream on top. So one should not try to remove all the cream out of the cake or it would be difficult to sell. So lets go back to that example again. If ground rent of 7 flat is 1750 and freehold is worth 20 to 24 time ground rent then what would be our profit?

Example:

Freehold and leasehold Title Splitting	
Beer Multipack	£500,000
Beer Cans £100000x10	£1,000,000
Cardboard Container (Freehold)	£45,000
Total Profit	£545,000

So that is what you would make. It is worth having that extra money. If you are doing bigger conversion you would have more money. This adds to the overall profit you would have in your commercial conversion project. So do not simply leave money on the table.

We bought the building for our client for £300000. We got 3 regulated flat, 2 came back and sold for £250,000 each and top floor

GUIDE TO COMMERCIAL PROPERTY CONVERSIONS
SPECIAL 3RD EDITION

development was sold with planning for £400,000. It was mainly a paper work exercise. We did not had to do much physically. These type of deals are out there and you just need to see them from a different angle. Imagine if you are simply making at least 5% extra by selling freeholder in every deal its worth making that money. So the bigger the deal you do the bigger the property is without doing much apart from creating some paper work. Well I am not saying you use my service and get rid of your solicitor, if you have good working relationship with your solicitors let them draft the lease what I can do for you to take their draft lease and put some clauses in their to enhance the freehold value. And I will give it back to them and they will check what I have put in to the lease is legal. That's what I do with my of my investor clients.

See the example below what we made from a freehold block deal:

Freehold and leasehold Title Splitting	
Purchase price of a block of 24 flats	£300,000
Cost to gain Planning on top floor	£25,000
Freehold Sold with planning	£400,000
Got 2 additional flat lease back	£500,000
Total Profit	£575,000
ROI %	176.92%

CHAPTER 10: THE BEST INVESTMENT

In my view the best investment is investing time and effort in your own education and personal development.

"The best investment you can make is in yourself"

Warren buffett

The knowledge and skills you gain through educations will stay with you for the rest of your life. Most of the people, the only education they get is the formal education they receive in school, college and university.

Unfortunately, this traditional form of education does not teach you the fundamentals of life about money, investing and creating business.

Since 1999, I have been investing my time and efforts in my own personal development. I am constantly improving myself, my skills and expertise every year and every month. I believe we should never stop leaning. I believe if you stop learning then you will feel as if life is moving slow. I am member of few professional bodies like Royal institute of chartered surveyor (RICS). As part of my professional membership we all need to

GUIDE TO COMMERCIAL PROPERTY CONVERSIONS
SPECIAL 3RD EDITION

get our annual CPD, however that's just to keep up to date within the field we are practicing. Likewise, for investing, things are changing so our strategies of investment have to be up to date all the time.

Without appearing to sound arrogant, I have been into real estate for over 20 years and having international property investment experience, yet I do not claim to know all about real estate. I learn something new every day. I am always looking to learn from other successful investors and improve on what I do.

I coached and trained many investors and I've tought complete bigginers to advance people with some experience. Unfortunately, when someone says or thinks "I know this" because they are closing down their mind to new possibilities and opportunity.

Many people are not prepared to put the time, effort or money into educating themselves. I must say, I was very skeptical before I got into personal development. But now, I think spending money to go on to seminar and events are worth because I know if I get just one good idea it will be worth time

GUIDE TO COMMERCIAL PROPERTY CONVERSIONS
SPECIAL 3RD EDITION

and money. Each year I commit to spend a certain amount of money and time developing myself further. I really enjoy learning and growing. I understand the value of paying for information and expertise.

I am very confident that, if I have to start again everything today, I would be able to get back to where I am now much quicker, faster and easier than I did the first time because I know exactly what to do this time and maybe more importantly what not to do. How about you? Are you investing enough in yourself? Do you have the right belief and do you think you have got right kills and knowldege and what it require to be successful property investor?

What skills do you need to be a successful investor?

Growth Mindset and right attitude: I firmly believe that you can have all the skills, knowledge and strategies in the world but these are useless if you don't have the right investor's mindset. To be a successful property investor you need to have the right attitude and self-belief that you can achieve anything you put your mind to. Most investors think that investing is all about the strategies and techniques you use. I personally believe that the strategies are 25% and your attitude and mindset are 75% of what it takes to be a really successful property investor.

Positive attitude: You are generally a positive or a negative person. I know we all go through phases and sometimes we have bad days but I promise you it is easier to achieve what you want if you are positive and looking for the possibilities rather looking for negatives and what can't be done. You get what you think about and focus on. As a property problem solver, you need to be very creative, with the solution-focused outlook. There is always a way. Your role is often to solve problem by finding solution that other people cannot see.

"Make your GOALS so big and inspiring that they make your problems seem insignificant by comparison."

Self-Discipline: To be a successful we something need to push ourselves and do things outside of our comfort zone. It can be very easy to use excuse as to why we have not done something, but really it just comes down to being disciplined and focus on

GUIDE TO COMMERCIAL PROPERTY CONVERSIONS
SPECIAL 3RD EDITION

what you want. We may need to make some short-term sacrifice in order to achieve and enjoy long-term benefits.

Having the discipline to do something each day to move you towards your goals will have a massive positive impact on your results.

Financial skills: Property investing is all about the numbers and return on investment. You need to be able to work out if a deal stacks up or not. Fortunately, you don't have to do this in your head or on the spot, but you do need to understand the numbers upon which you will base your investing decisions. To help people I offer free property deal analyser on my website at www.propertyexpertsacademy.com you can download it for free.

Negotiation skills: As I always maintain throughout this book you need to come up with a solution that is win/win for both you and the seller. You need to be ethical and make sure that you don't take advantage of the sellers' situation. Having said this, the deal has to work for you otherwise there's no point doing it. Remember, this is a business. In most motivated seller purchases there is some scope for negotiation. The level of your negotiation skills can dramatically impact the profitability of your business.

Understanding and Listening skills: The best way to help a motivated seller is to ask them what they want and listen to what they tell you. As simple as this sound, all too often I hear of investors who talk at motivated sellers rather than talking with them. Building rapport and the trusting relationship is very critical if you want to help these people and secure a good win/win deal. You need to become good at asking question and listening to the answers to make sure you really understand the situation and find the best possible solution for you and the motivated seller.

"Understand the problem of seller and wrap your offer around it"

Research & Analysis skills: Whenever you find a potential motivated seller lead, you need to act very quickly. Before you move on any deal, you need to quickly assess whether it will work for you. Research is very important. You need to be able to determine the value of a property, the rental potential and

GUIDE TO COMMERCIAL PROPERTY CONVERSIONS
SPECIAL 3RD EDITION

realistic rental income that it might achieve. Fortunately, it is extremely easy and quick to do this with the use of the internet these days and the telephone few local agents and experts. You would notice, it can take just 20 to 30 minutes to obtain an estimated valuation that a chartered surveyor would also arrive at using like comparison of similar properties.

Persistence: This is one of the most important skills you can develop. Investing in property is not easy. There are lots of challenges and obstacles you will need to overcome. Your rewards are many times directly linked with these challenges. Unfortunately most people give up for too easily, often just before they achieve the results they are looking for. You need to keep going and remember that if other people have been successful and found a way there is no reason why you can't do the same.

"Fall down 10 times, get up 11th time"

Looking at your current skills set compare to the skills required to be a successful property problem solver, where do you feel that you may need to improve your skills? What can you do to improve your skills?

GUIDE TO COMMERCIAL PROPERTY CONVERSIONS
SPECIAL 3RD EDITION

Remember, you don't have to be good at everything. You can get other people to help you in areas in which you are not so strong. Working with other people is much smarter than doing it on your own, which can be very lonely.

Be smart and Educate yourself smartly

Now that we have recognized the need to constantly improve yourself and develop your skills, knowledge and experience, there are several ways in which you can achieve this. You need to select the methods that best fit with your time and personal requirements. Here are a few ideas for you:

Right company and Networking: There are now many very good networking group for property investors in all over the country and world. Attending this event on a regular basis is one of the best ways to develop your knowledge by mixing with and learning from other successful investors. I recognized the incredible value that I had personally gained by learning from and networking with other successful investors. Networking is a low-cost way of gaining knowledge in terms of financial requirements, but it does require some time, effort and dedication from you.

GUIDE TO COMMERCIAL PROPERTY CONVERSIONS
SPECIAL 3RD EDITION

The more investors you know and the bigger your network is, the more opportunities you will become aware of. There are property investors groups all over the UK. I suggest you use the internet to find a group near to where you live or work and start visiting on a regular basis. This is also a great way to keep yourself motivated and on track. Property investing can be lonely sometimes, especially if your friends and family don't really understand what you do. You need to be around like minded people who can give your support, encouragement and advice.

Educational seminar and courses: there are number of individuals and companies in the UK who provide property investment education. Some of them are better than others and it is up to you to decide which is best one for you. Seminars are a great way for you to learn a lot of information very quickly. Although you often have to pay to attend these seminars, the knowledge that you gain will make the investment of time and money very worthwhile. I do offer free seminars many times in the year. Look at my website

GUIDE TO COMMERCIAL PROPERTY CONVERSIONS
SPECIAL 3RD EDITION

www.propertyexpertsacademey.com for details or subscribe for such information.

To be honest, given enough time and research, you could probably discover for yourself most of the information that you will learn on a seminar. However the main reason you attend a seminar is to obtain a lot of information, compressed into very short amount of time.

Coaches or mentors: Reading books or attending seminars to learn how to invest in property is pointless unless you put your knowledge into practice. One of the best ways of doing this is to have a coach who will support you, help you to take action and hold you to account. Your coach should be someone who is more experience than you and can add value to investing, help you to grow and expand your knowledge.

My group of companies, provide almost anything that you would need in your property investment journey. If you like to be mentored by us and need any help in your property investment journey, please visit our website and fill up your details with your requirement. I and my team would be more than happy to work with you. I work with motivated and ambitious people just

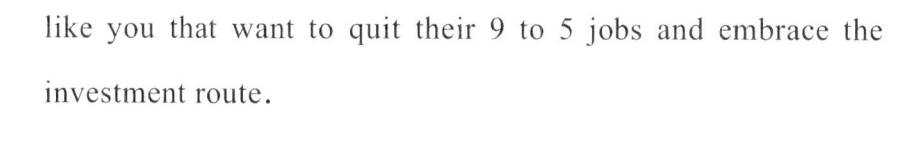

GUIDE TO COMMERCIAL PROPERTY CONVERSIONS
SPECIAL 3RD EDITION

like you that want to quit their 9 to 5 jobs and embrace the investment route.

GUIDE TO COMMERCIAL PROPERTY CONVERSIONS
SPECIAL 3RD EDITION

Top Tips & Dos & Don'ts

Here are some top tips and some dos and don'ts for investing in property using your money:

1) Invest locally. Get to know your local (highest demand) area and your returns, control and cash flow will increase.

2) Leverage your funds with bank finance to get 500% more cash on cash returns.

3) Buy cheaper properties (middle ground with capital growth) with higher yields (cash flow) and lower risk.

4) Don't go in blind. Get educated, do your research and diligence, do the numbers stack and make financial sense towards your property goals?

5) Create multiple streams of income from different property types such as single-let, multi-let and commercial property conversions.

6) Utilize the many new government tax-saving strategies, such a permitted development, commerical to residential conversion and capital allowances etc.

GUIDE TO COMMERCIAL PROPERTY CONVERSIONS
SPECIAL 3RD EDITION

7) Shop around for the best mortgage. Don't just walk to your nearest high street but speak to a reputable independent mortgage broker who will advise and get you the best deals.

8) Know the pitfalls. Have cash buffer for rate rise large maintenance bills or longer than expected void periods.

9) Start now. It's never too late to start but always too late to wait.

ABOUT SUMIT GUPTA

AssocRICS B.Com (Hons) PGDBA (FINANCE) MBA (INTERNATIONAL BUSINESS)

An entrepreneur, Author, Property Investor & Mentor

Sumit Gupta is founder of Property Experts Academy, Global Property Consulting and several other ventures. He has been advising clients and mentoring property investors for over a decade. Sumit Gupta also has helped 100s of people to successfully build their property portfolios.

Sumit Gupta, through his company Global Property Consulting is specialize in advising clients on Investment and disposal, landlord and tenant disputes, lease extension valuation and commercial property rent review, lease renewals, dilapidations and capital allowances claims.

GUIDE TO COMMERCIAL PROPERTY CONVERSIONS
SPECIAL 3RD EDITION

He also acts as Expert witness and Joint Expert witness for various reputed clients in London. He represents clients in tribunal, upper tribunal, court and High court.

Sumit Gupta training programs have been delivered in the UK and India.

Meet Sumit Gupta and receive world-class property investment training at www.propertyexpertsacademy.com

We like to thanks our below sponsors Partners

GUIDE TO COMMERCIAL PROPERTY CONVERSIONS
SPECIAL 3RD EDITION

Success Resources Ventures is the fastest growing training company in the world.

At SRV, we offer various training from wealth training to life coaching, such as Property investment training, forex training, public speaking training, book writing training. Online marketing, business training and many more.

To know more visit us at www.successresourcesventures.com

GUIDE TO COMMERCIAL PROPERTY CONVERSIONS
SPECIAL 3RD EDITION

Property Experts Academy teaches the various S.T.R.A.T.E.G.I.E.S ™ that can help anyone to successfully invest in property and achieve financial freedom.

S – Sell leads (deal packaging)

T- Title splitting

R- Rent To Rent

A- Auction purchase using special techniques

T- To Let (buy to Let)

E- Exchange with delay completion

GUIDE TO COMMERCIAL PROPERTY CONVERSIONS
SPECIAL 3RD EDITION

G- Get control by taking option or lease option

I- Internal Conversion including commercial conversion

E- Extra accommodation for multiple tenants (HMO)

S- Service Accommodation and Holiday let

To know more visit us at www.propertyexpertsacademy.com

GUIDE TO COMMERCIAL PROPERTY CONVERSIONS
SPECIAL 3RD EDITION

Over the past decades, GPC has emerged as one of the leading independent consultancy. Renowned for applying the highest standards of quality and integrity in all our property services.

We are passionate about Real Estate and are consummately professional in everything we do, which is why we are the fastest growing privately owned property consultancy company.

We are specialise in Investment, Rent Reviews, lease renewal, lease extension and lease enfranchisement valuation and negotiations.
To know more visit us at www.global-property-consulting.com

GUIDE TO COMMERCIAL PROPERTY CONVERSIONS
SPECIAL 3RD EDITION

PROPERTY SOLUTIONS COMPANY
WE BUY ANY PROPERTY

Over last 15 years, PSC has emerged as one of the leading independent consultancy. Renowned for applying the highest standards of quality and integrity in all our property services.

We are passionate about Real Estate and are consummately professional in everything we do, which is why we are the fastest growing privately owned property consultancy company.

We are property problem solver, and we can buy any property regardless of any situation or condition.

To know more visit us at www.propertysolutionsco.uk

GUIDE TO COMMERCIAL PROPERTY CONVERSIONS
SPECIAL 3RD EDITION

WARNING!
THIS BOOK READING COULD CHANGE YOUR DESTINY AND SHAPE YOUR FUTURE EVEN BETTER

A GUIDE TO COMMERCIAL PROPERTY CONVERSION WILL TEACH YOU THE MOST INNOVATIVE TECHNIQUES YOU CAN USE IN ANY MARKET CONDITION OR GEOGRAPHIC AREA. SUMIT GUPTA, THROUGH THIS BOOK, WILL SHOW YOU HOW TO MAKE BIG PROFIT BY FINDING COMMERCIAL PROPERTY AND TURNING THEM INTO RESIDENTIAL PROPERTIES.

POWERFUL TECHNIQUES ANYONE CAN USE TO REPLACE THEIR SALARY AND ESCAPE THE RAT RACE QUICKLY. THIS BOOK SHOWS YOU HOW TO INVEST EVEN IF YOU HAVE NONE OF YOUR OWN MONEY TO INVEST

SUMIT GUPTA IS AN INTERNATIONALLY KNOWN PROPERTY EXPERT, AUTHOR, ENTREPRENEUR, PROPERTY INVESTOR & MENTOR WHO HAS BOUGHT, CONTROL AND SOLD OVER 500 PROPERTIES ALL TOGETHER OVER LAST 17 YEARS WORLDWIDE.

DISCOVER MORE ABOUT THE AUTHOR AND HIS PROPERTY INVESTMENT TRAINING PROGRAMS AT WWW.PROPERTYEXPERTSACADEMY.COM

Sumit Gupta
AssocRICS B.Com (Hons) PGDBA (FINANCE) MBA (INTERNATIONAL BUSINESS)
An entrepreneur, Author, Property Investor & Mentor

Printed in Great Britain
by Amazon